The Xenophobe's Guide to The English

Antony Miall

RAVETTE BOOKS

Published by Ravette Books Limited
P O Box 296
Horsham
West Sussex RH13 8FH
Tel: & Fax: (01 403) 711443

First printed 1993
Revised 1994

Editor – Alison Coles
Series Editor – Anne Tauté

Cover designer – Jim Wire
Printer – Cox & Wyman Ltd.
Producer – Oval Projects Ltd.

An Oval Project
for Ravette Books Ltd.

Contents

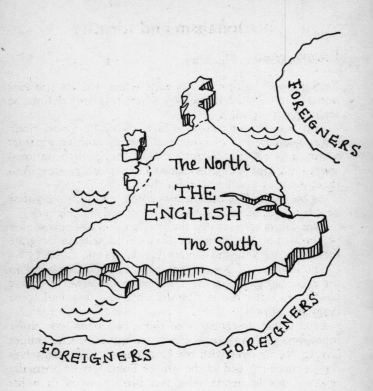

'The English have a natural distrust of the unfamiliar and nowhere is this more clearly seen than in their attitude to the geography of their own country.'

The English population is just over 48 million (compared with 5 million Danes, 8½ million Swedish, 15 million Dutch, 39 million Spanish, 57 million French, 57 million Italians and 80 million Germans).

Nationalism and Identity

Forewarned

Xenophobia*, although a Greek word, has its spiritual home in the English dictionary where it is drily defined as an 'abstract' noun.

This is misleading. It is, in fact, a very 'common' noun – an everyday sort of noun really, with nothing abstract about it at all. For xenophobia is the English national sport – England's most enduring cultural expression. And there is a very good reason for that.

. As far as the English are concerned, all of life's greatest problems can be summed up in one word – foreigners.

Nine hundred years ago the last invasion of England was perpetrated by the Normans. They settled, tried to integrate themselves with the indigenous population and failed.

The indigenous population then, as now, displayed an utter contempt for them not merely because they had conquered but more importantly because they had come from abroad.

Even today descendants of those Normans who think to impress with a throw-away remark about their families having "come over with the Conqueror" find themselves on the receiving end of the sort of English frost normally reserved for someone who has broken wind in a lift between floors.

The real English deal with them as they dealt with the Romans, the Phoenicians, the Celts, Jutes, Saxons and, more recently, every other nation on earth (especially the French) – with polite but firm disdain.

*Actually the English prefer 'xenolipi' (pity for foreigners) but both words, being foreign in origin, are of limited pertinence in any case.

The whole thing is rather like cricket, the archetypal English game. It lasts all your life and it is apparently more important to play than to win – a sentiment which is more reminiscent of Confucius than Carruthers.

That is what you are up against. It is useless to imagine that you can succeed where so many have failed. But since it is the proudest English boast that they cannot begin to understand foreigners, it would be gratifying to steal a march on them by beginning to understand *them*.

How They See Others

English views on foreigners are very simple. The further one travels from the capital in any direction, the more outlandish the people become.

When it comes to their neighbours in the British Isles, the English are in absolutely no doubt as to their own innate superiority. This they see as no petty prejudice but rather as a scientific observation. The Irish are perceived as being wildly eccentric at best, completely mad at worst. The Welsh are dishonest and the Scots are dour and mean.

However, the Irish, Welsh and Scots should take heart. For most English they are not quite as appalling as their cousins across the Channel. They should also remember that 'foreign-ness' for the English starts to a certain extent at the end of their own street.

The French and the English have been sparring partners for so long that the English have developed a kind of love-hate relationship with them. The English love France. They love its food and wine and thoroughly approve of its climate. There is a subconscious historical belief that the French have no right to be living in France at all, to the extent that thousands of Englishmen try annually to turn the more attractive areas of France into little corners of Surrey.

As to the French people, they are perceived as insincere, unhygienic and given to sexual excess.

With the Germans the English are less equivocal. Germans are megalomaniac, easily-led bullies who have not even the saving grace of culinary skill.

Conveniently forgetting the fact that their own Royal family is of German descent, the English make no pretence at liking the Germans. Confronted with one, they will constantly be reminding themselves 'not to mention the War' whilst secretly wondering whether he or she is old enough to have fought in it.

For the rest of Europe, as far as the English are concerned, the Italians are hysterical and dishonest; the Spanish, lazy; the Russians, gloomy; and the Scandinavians, Dutch, Belgians and Swiss, dull. Further afield English odium is no less concentrated. Americans and Australians are vulgar, Canadians are boring, and all oriental peoples inscrutable and dangerous.

You will only find this out, of course, by listening at keyholes, for to your face they will always be charming. They appear to be tolerant to a fault. In actuality, they only value foreigners for their backs – which they can use for talking behind.

Special Relationships

The English have a natural distrust of the unfamiliar and nowhere is this more clearly seen than in their attitude to the geography of their own country.

Since time immemorial there has been a North-South

divide in England. To the Southerner, civilization ends somewhere around Potters Bar (just north of London). Beyond that point, he believes, the inhabitants are all ruddier in complexion, more hirsute and blunt to the point of rudeness. These traits he generously puts down to the cooler climate.

In the North they frighten their children to sleep with tales of the deviousness of the inhabitants 'down South.' They point to their softness, their mucked-about food and their airy-fairiness on all matters of real importance. Nevertheless, *any* English man or woman, no matter how soft or hairy, is entitled to special treatment as, to a lesser extent, are the inhabitants of those countries which represent the English conscience – once the Empire, now the shrinking Commonwealth.

How Others See Them

To outsiders the English are intellectually impenetrable. They express little emotion. They are not so much slow as stationary to anger and the pleasures of life seem to pass them by as they revel in discomfort and self-denial.

Their culinary appreciation is incomprehensible to most, but especially the French, and in their hesitation to be direct or state a view, they are rarely understood.

With an unparalleled sense of historical continuity, they appear to carry on in their own sweet way largely unmoved by developments in the world around them. The unlikely effect of all this is that outsiders have a kind of grudging respect for them. This is partly because they amuse, and partly because they are consistent.

Fascinatingly ghastly they may be, but you know just where you are with them.

How They See Themselves

The English don't just believe themselves superior to all other nations. They also believe that all other nations secretly know that they are.

They feel themselves to be natural leaders, the most obvious choice for 'top nation'. Geography reinforces this belief as the inhabitants look out to the sea all around them from the fastness of their 'tight little island'. Nobody would ever question the aptness of the newspaper report: 'Fog in the Channel – Continent cut off.'

With their wealth of experience of 'running the show', as they see it, they are also deeply aware of their responsibilities to others. These they take very seriously, which means that throughout life they act rather like head boys or head girls in school. They see it as their solemn duty to protect the weak, strengthen the faint-hearted and shame bullies into submission. These are their roles in life and they fulfil them, by and large, to their entire satisfaction.

How They Would Like to be Seen

Although it is impossible for the English to appear to care what others think of them, deep down they would like to be loved and appreciated for what they see as the sterling qualities they possess. These qualities, which they bring selflessly to the world forum, include a reflex action which leads them to champion the underdog and treat persecutors with a firm hand, absolute truthfulness and a commitment never to break a promise or to go back on one's word.

In a perfect world, the English suspect everyone would be more like them. Then, and only then, would they achieve the recognition and affection they feel they so richly deserve.

Character

Stiff Upper Lip

The characteristic English pose involves keeping the head held high, the upper lip stiff and the best foot forward. In this position, conversation is difficult and intimacy of any kind almost impossible. This in itself is a clue to the English character.

Puritanism

Puritanism has always found in the English its most fertile breeding ground. For hundreds of years their children have been brainwashed with trite little sayings – "Silence is golden", "Empty vessels make the most noise" and, most telling,"You are not put on to this earth to enjoy yourself".

Small wonder that they end up, as adults, acting rather like the three wise monkeys and emotionally in traction.

But still the English defend their character and behaviour against all comers. Perhaps that is because Puritanism with its punishing work ethic assures them that their reward for all that restraint will come at a sort of school prize-giving ceremony in the world to come.

If it is the latter, they are forgetting that since God is also English – a firmly-held belief – any hedonism in the next world will probably be accompanied by mugs of bromide.

Nevertheless, the English continue to bask in this certainty to the general astonishment of the rest of mankind.

Moderation

If there is one trait that absolutely singles out the English it is their shared dislike for anyone or anything that 'goes too far'.

Going too far, as the English see it, covers displaying an excess of emotion, getting drunk, discussing money in public or cracking off-colour jokes and then laughing at them noisily. Beyond the pale altogether is the man or woman who regales one with his or her titles or qualifications. The only acceptable place to air these is on an envelope.

To the English the proper way to behave in almost all situations is to display a languid indifference to almost everything, though one may be seething underneath. Even in affairs of the heart, it is considered unseemly to show one's feelings except behind closed doors.

A Good Sport

If an English man or woman refers to you as 'a good sport', you will know that you have really arrived. For to them it is a qualification normally never awarded to a foreigner and by no means within the grasp of all the English.

The term is not exclusively a sporting one. It describes the sort of behaviour both on and off the playing field that characterises everything the English really respect. In all physical trials, the good sport will play without having been seen to practise too hard and will, ideally, win from innate superiority. He or she will then be dismissive of their victory and magnanimous towards the loser.

It goes without saying that the good sport will also be a good loser. There will be no arguing with umpires or outward signs of disappointment. On the contrary, a remark such as "The best man won!" tossed airily to all and sundry, and never through clenched teeth, is obligatory even in the face of crushing defeat.

This does not really fool anyone, for the English are fiercely competitive especially in matters sporting. They would rather be crossed in love than beaten on the tennis courts, but to let it be seen would be going too far.

Self-doubt

It is the apparent colossal self-confidence and moral certainty of the English that is paradoxically one of their greatest stumbling blocks. For both qualities are, to a certain extent, only illusions. Whilst they may appear fearless and calm on the surface, deep down the English suffer from agonising self-doubt, feeling that in many areas of human activity they just cannot cut the mustard.

All the time there were countries to be conquered and foreigners to be governed, the English could sublimate all their clamouring uncertainty. The scent of success served as incense at the altar of their self-assurance.

But with the helter-skelter slide from Empire to Commonwealth and ever downwards, their doubts, like itches, have begun to plague them and it is considered bad form to scratch in public.

Sentiment

The English have a strong sense of history. Because their past was so infinitely more glamorous than their present, they cling to it tenaciously. Mix this love of bygone ages with an unrivalled sentimentality and you have a heady mixture which can be sensed in every aspect of the English life.

Antique shops clutter up every town and village. English homes are filled with old things not only because they please the eye but because there is a feeling that anything that has stood the test of time must be better than its modern counterpart.

The English generally distrust the new-fangled or modern. Shininess is vulgar and the patina of age lends respectability. Thus they cling on to old furniture, old carpets, old chipped china, old kitchen gadgets and garden implements long after common sense dictates that they should be replaced.

"If it was good enough for my grandfather/grandmother, it's good enough for me!" The English cry goes up and each new invasion from the future is greeted with the indignant question: "What was wrong with the old one?"

And as far as the English are concerned, there is no answer to that.

Inventiveness

The English are endlessly resourceful and inventive, but rarely profit from their inventions. The inventor in his garden shed turning out gadgets and widgets tends to be almost exclusively male, lacking the more practical female genes in any great numbers.

Often perceiving needs in daily life which have gone unobserved by the rest of his compatriots, he will beaver away 24 hours a day creating such indispensable items as the perfect egg boiler or the self-creasing trouser.

Occasionally, though, he will come up with something with real promise like the hovercraft which will then be ignored by his countrymen and taken up by foreigners.

Attitudes and Values

The English are governed by a simple set of attitudes and values to which everyone pays lip service, whether they believe in them or not. There is, however, one exception to this rule and that is:

Common Sense

Common sense is central to the English attitude to almost everything in life. It is common sense to carry an umbrella in case of rain. It is common sense not to sit on cold stone (which bestows haemorrhoids). It is common sense to wear clean underwear in case one is run over and taken to hospital.

In fact, it is common sense and thoroughly English never to be wrong-footed in any way. To fall foul of changing circumstances is inexcusable. One should 'be prepared' at all times.

For the English, common sense is part of the historical imperative. It was common sense that beat back the Armada and won the Empire. The lack of it caused the Fall of Troy, the French Revolution and almost any other foreign debacle you care to mention.

It is common sense that sets the English apart: they may look silly in their plastic macs on the Riviera, but the last laugh will be on them if the Mistral comes early.

Of course it does not always work; sometimes germs do get through despite their efforts. Then, as well as looking ridiculous, they sport that archetypal affliction, 'le sang-froid habituel des Anglais' – the English person's usual bloody cold.

Class

Belonging is important to the English. Individuality is all very well, in some cases it can be commendable, but, on the whole, being part of a team is their preferred situation and they are never happier than when they are surrounded by a group of people with whom they either have, or affect to have, everything in common.

This urge for togetherness manifests itself in many ways. Historically its most obvious symptom is found in the English devotion to the class system which is central to the whole English way of life. Its importance can hardly be overrated and it should never be dismissed. It is the unseen joker in the pack – the card that negates or validates the whole game of life and turns winners into losers and vice versa.

The class system is a reflection of the fierce competitiveness of the English. For whilst they believe that, as a race, they are superior to every other nation on earth, they have a surprising need to establish their individual superiority within their own society. They do this by manoeuvring themselves into cliques in whose company they feel comfortable. Once there, they adopt mutually exclusive fashions of all kinds and nurture a kind of phobia about other groupings to which they do not belong. All this is achieved through skilful manipulation of the class code.

The existence of the class system is a living proof of the English devotion to tradition, their innate fear of their own inferiority and their desire to better themselves in the eyes of their compatriots. The whole thing can appear to be of paramount importance but there is also, ironically, something of the game about it. Like all English games it is more important to play, than to win.

English tradition demands the existence of three classes.

Once upon a time these equated to the old groupings of aristocracy, merchants and workers. However, with the irresistible rise of the merchant or middle class, the aristocracy and workers were squeezed out of the frame and the middle class turned its attention to dividing itself into an upper, middle, and lower class. Around 98% of the English are, in fact, middle class.

The aristocracy, representing barely 1% of the population, is historically above joining in the class game although it still serves as the arbiter of it. The working class is now pretty well extinct and today represents at most 1% of the population. For them the whole social game is beneath contempt. Thus it is left to the middle class to provide all the players.

However much English class structures change, class consciousness never disappears. When BBC interviewer Sandra Harris met that beldame of letters, Dame Barbara Cartland, in the 1960s, she asked her: "Have English class barriers broken down?" Dame Barbara, with saccharine honesty, assured her: "Of course they have, or I wouldn't be sitting here talking to someone like you."

The Dame was, of course, exaggerating. Class barriers still exist and competition to scramble over them ahead of one's compatriots is fierce.

Because of this, the middle-class English can never relax. They are conscious that in every aspect of life they must project the 'right' image – one based on their perception of what their betters would cultivate if they had to bother. They care desperately about what they wear, what they say, what they eat and drink, where they live and with whom they are seen.

It is an exhausting business because there is so much at stake. For while it is almost impossible to move down a class, a glorious upward bound can be achieved provided the player does not make a single false move when on trial. And, of course, social life is nothing if not a succession of trials for the middle-class English.

Trial by Conversation

The English attach enormous importance to accents. Nowadays a regional drawl is not necessarily a fatal flaw but what used to be called an 'Oxford' accent or 'BBC' pronunciation will still stand the accused in the best stead. Probably even more important than vowel sounds is vocabulary. Traditionally the upper classes have always agreed with the working classes that a spade should be called a spade and never a garden implement.

Although they are adept at avoiding saying what they actually mean, the words the well-bred English use to conceal their real feelings are preferably direct. They never use foreign words when there are perfectly good English ones for the same things (i.e. napkin and not serviette). Short Anglo-Saxon words are used to describe bodily functions. All euphemism is anathema and hyper-delicacy, abhorrent.

This makes life tricky for the middle classes who confuse delicacy with refinement and tend to avoid any direct confrontation with what they perceive to be coarse or vulgar. Until they learn to refer to 'lunch' not 'dinner' at lunchtime, sit in the 'sitting room' rather than the 'lounge', on a 'sofa and chairs', not a '3-piece suite', go to the 'loo' not the 'toilet', and use 'scent' rather than 'perfume', they can never pass the conversation test.

The most important single word in the social climber's vocabulary is 'common'. It should be used frequently to describe anyone or anything which offends one's assumed level of sensibility. There is no appeal against 'commonness'.

Trial by Table Manners

The English have a growing interest in food but it is the ritual of meals and table manners which hold an unrivalled fascination for them. This means that mealtimes are probably the most testing times for any player.

If the meal starts with soup, remember the English maritime tradition and tip the bowl away from you to avoid the soup spilling on to your lap in the event of a swell. And note that a knife should not be held like a pencil and that 'pudding' is never 'sweet' except adjectivally.

Trial by Dress

The English are, understandably, primarily concerned with keeping warm and admonish impractical fashion victims that they will 'catch their death of cold'.

Predictably, upper-class fashions mostly reflect tradition. The natural habitat of the English gentleman or woman is the country, not the town, and this is reflected in their wardrobe. Preferred colours, dismal browns and duns, remind them of their estates and often bring a whiff of the Borders to the West End of London, where green Wellington boots and Barbour shooting jackets are not considered any more out of place than four-wheel drive Range Rovers.

For while fashion itself is transitory, the English way of life goes on for ever. So, it sometimes seems, do English clothes. Formal outfits have to be bought on occasion, but they should never look new. Neither should old school, regimental or club ties. Casual clothes are chosen for their comfort, not for their appearance.

Fashion, even foreign fashion, interests the English increasingly, and this is reflected in a growing awareness of cut and style. However, no designer can change the

Englishman's penchant for trousers which are a little too short for the leg, as if he had somehow grown out of them.

Trial by Love

Love is something that does not come all that naturally to the English, who see romanticism as a threat to practicality and common sense. In terms of the social climb, however, it is central. It is, after all, the one way in which one can move upwards in one bound. A good marriage can put a social climber in a commanding position. But in the game of life, even the English acknowledge that the love card is wild. That is why they are so wary of it.

Conclusion

If you come through the trials and establish your credentials, you may earn a grudging respect in English social circles.

Finally, though, the laugh is on you. For if you have really had to try, you have lost. The accused in this trial needs to exercise every care except, perhaps, that of caring too much.

Sex

It is hard to believe that the English reproduce, for while other nations celebrate their sexuality, to a greater or lesser extent, the English regard theirs as the enemy within.

The sexually-unattractive Oliver Cromwell and the Puritans in general have got a lot to answer for. Together they drove the issue underground hundreds of years ago and it has been growing there ever since quietly choking the flower of English youth and occasionally upsetting the entire garden plan.

But instead of ploughing up the whole area, the English have played around with trowels and forks for centuries. Consequently they have never, so to speak, solved the problem.

This is strange, for the English are fearless in their confrontation of almost everything else. In all other matters emotional or psychological, while angels hover nervously on the sidelines, the practical English rush in, dragging their tea urns behind them, ready to cope. When it comes to sex, however, they are struck dumb and stumble about helplessly.

Because of their inclination to ignore the existence of the sexual impulse, the English have never really seen sex as a fit subject for study or discussion. The result is that their attitudes towards it are still characterised by the superstitions, myths and taboos of less enlightened ages. In consequence, many English see sex in terms of domination – a liaison being termed a 'conquest' of one party by the other.

When it comes to the act itself, the English have always felt themselves to be inferior practitioners. As far as men and women are concerned, sex was, and to a certain extent still is, primarily about reproduction. Lights out, face to face, is the name of the game.

It is as well, too, to remember that for the English, even sex is not free of class distinction. Tradition has it, for example, that the sign of a gentleman is that he will take his own weight on his elbows and, however, intimate the moment, he will always remember to thank his hostess for having him, just as she will thank him for coming.

Voyeurism is a favourite hobby. The English love to read about sex. Newspapers are full of the bedtime exploits of others and the peccadillos of the famous are a constant thrill. Nothing, even the act itself, can enthral the English quite as much as reading about some sado-masochistic pillar of society caught bending over in Bayswater on a Sunday afternoon.

But safer, and perhaps even more to the English taste, is sexual innuendo of the seaside postcard kind. Naturally nervous of sex, they feel happiest when they are tittering about it. So it's Benny Hill and 'Carry on Bottom' for a really good night out – followed by a comforting anaphrodisiac – a few too many lagers or a mug of steaming cocoa.

Wealth and Success

The English generally prefer the old to the new in their daily life and dislike change in the status of their relatives and acquaintances.

'Old' money is preferable to 'new' money and inherited money is infinitely preferable to money earned. Those who suddenly achieve wealth are referred to dismissively and anyone who talks about their financial status or hints that he or she might be anything more than 'comfortably off', will get a very cool reception in desirable social circles.

Overt enjoyment or the flaunting of wealth is also considered rather bad form and the innate puritanism of the English warns 'Pools' winners that no good will come of their having won and that "money cannot buy happiness".

Unlike their transatlantic cousins, the English have an inherent distrust of success and look upon money with disdain. Misquoting the Bible to underline this attitude, they aver that: "Money is the root of all evil." What they really mean is that everybody else's is.

Behaviour

The Family

Annual holidays apart, the English do not tend to spend much time with their families. Once the tiresome business of childhood is over, they set out on life's journey largely unhampered by considerations of siblings or parents. Free at last, they can apply themselves to cultivating that most English talent – not getting on with others – and to starting their own uncommunicative families.

Children

Anyone who has tried to get lunch for a small child in a pub on Dartmoor in the depths of winter, will know the despair that clutches the heart at the sight of that notice – 'No Children, No Dogs.'

Although the two nuisances are lumped together in this instance, they are seldom mentioned in the same breath for while most English people like dogs, not many of them like children.

Children make them nervous. They are unpredictable. Where should they patted ? On the head, perhaps: "Well, well, my little man – and what do you want to be when you grow up?"

The implication of the question is clear. An English childhood is something to be got over as quickly as possible. To be an English grown-up – that is the only really glorious thing. No wonder the English child is in such a hurry to be one.

English embarrassment about sex is nothing to the embarrassment they show about its consequences. Pregnancy is not considered a fit topic for conversation.

The sooner a mother is back on her feet (or back) after childbirth the better and, despite the best efforts of feminism, breast-feeding is still seen as almost as private a bodily function as the others.

Only when the baby is beautifully dressed in a christening robe will the English outside the immediate family deign to acknowledge its existence. Then they will tell it that it looks just like its mother or father – never like itself.

Animals

It is an English maxim that a person who likes animals cannot be all bad for the English adore animals – all kinds of animals. They keep them, not, as other nations do, primarily to guard their property, for scientific interest or for status, but for company.

For while they are not always very good at talking to each other, they excel in conversation with their animals. Although they are not often successful at forming tactile bonds with their children, they continually chuck the chins of their lap dogs and whisper sweet nothings into their hairy ears.

This is because, unlike people, the wretched things cannot answer back. If they could the English might learn quite a lot about themselves. As it is, they are assumed to be in total agreement with their masters and mistresses and consequently enjoy an unrivalled position in the English affection.

Pet owners' homes are shrines to their animals. The best seats, the warmest spots, the choicest morsels are handed over to these household gods as a matter of course.

Cats and dogs, parrots and guinea pigs are excused

behaviour which if seen in the children of the household might well end in assault. They are deemed, by their owners, to be incapable of almost any misdemeanour. So when dog bites man, it is always man's fault, even if he is just a passer-by. Everyone in the vicinity will sympathize with the owner's disclaimer: "Fang wouldn't hurt a fly!"

Elders

The English, by and large, find their elderly as difficult to deal with as their children. An awkward minority group, they are often ignored by their families and, funds permitting, banged up in twilight homes. Every so often they will be visited by their relations who check that they are basically healthy and happy and that the security systems are in good order.

Other races find this attitude puzzling. To them the idea of the extended family with its inherent benefits for all generations is the norm. It is not for the English. With their children at school of and their old people out of harm's way, they can get on with the real business of life, with which, they believe, neither youth nor old age is equipped to cope.

Eccentrics

To the rest of the world the entire English race is eccentric. To the English themselves, the concept of eccentricity is a useful way of coping with the problem of anti-social or un-English behaviour in one of their own kind. Solidarity dictates that all the English, whether sane or not, are basically good eggs and worth any ten foreigners at twice the price.

So, to a certain extent, the English cultivate the idea of eccentricity as agreeable and even admirable.

The phenomenon of the eccentric does exist in its own right. Class and money have a lot to do with it. Mental affliction, usually described as lunacy in the poor, is grandly referred to as eccentricity in the rich.

It is all a question of scale. Thus non-threatening dotty behaviour, such as Lord Berners' predilection for travelling about the country in a motor-drawn horsebox filled with butterflies, and playing a grand piano, was met with a kind of admiration. He was, after all, a Lord.

The builders of batty follies and underground ballrooms are considered eccentric and applauded provided they spend enough money on their creations.

All these eccentrics are excused *de facto* from many of the conventions of correct English conduct.

However enjoyable they are, eccentrics do represent an element of danger to the English, for they flout convention. So to have a few is all very well, but only a few.

Immigrants

The English have always been among the first to accept refugees from less enlightened countries. But they do not see why any immigrant should expect to become part of the community within a matter of days, months or even years of their arrival. Any such ease of assimilation would, after all, fly in the face of the thousands of years it has taken to produce England and the English proper.

They are, however, generally a tolerant people, their attitude to minority groups being kindly if condescending. Anyone visiting an English town cannot fail to be aware of the rich mix of nationalities on view. This is because the English are better hosts to foreigners than most other nations. They are used to having aliens about the place and usually accord them just enough civility to make their lives bearable.

In many ways foreigners are treated rather like English children. That is to say they are seen, but not heard.

Manners and Etiquette

It is generally believed that the English are more formal than they really are. In fact, in day-to-day contact with each other they are less inclined to formality than the French or the Germans.

Perhaps it is the awesome spectacle of their state occasions that has given rise to the popularly held belief that even husbands and wives call each other by their titles and surnames. In reality, first names are commonly used among colleagues, and the American habit of using these on the telephone even before the names have met is now widespread.

The custom of men deferring to women is now somewhat on the wane, thanks to the strenuous efforts of the apostles of political correctness who see it more as condescension than consideration. You will, however, probably still get away with opening a door or giving up a seat for all but the most strident of feminists. But it is no longer de rigueur to jump to your feet when a woman enters the room, whether or not there are enough chairs.

Do Not Touch

However informal they are in their manner or address, when it comes to physical contact, the English are still deeply reserved.

They are not a tactile people. When greeting each other, men will shake hands on a first meeting but probably avoid doing so on subsequent ones. The preferred English handshake is a brief, vigorous affair with no hint of lingering. The cue question, "How do you do?" and the answer "How do you do?" signal the end of the ritual and hands should be crisply withdrawn from contact. Any deviation from the above procedure can cause all sorts of problems and suspicions of freemasonry, or worse.

Women may kiss on one or both cheeks; if they do, the miss-kiss is preferred – the kisser making a kissing gesture with appropriate sound-effects in the air in the general region of the recipient's ear or ears.

Men may kiss women in greeting, but only on the cheek. Trying to get a kiss on both cheeks can be risky as most women only expect the one, do not turn their heads for the second and receive it full frontally, which can result in the worst being feared – i.e. that it was an intentional ploy – an osculatory rape.

Most Englishmen never hug or (perish the thought) kiss other men. They leave that to football players and foreigners.

In public places, the English make strenuous efforts not to touch strangers even by accident. If such an accident should occur, apologies are fulsome but should never be used as an excuse for further conversation. On crowded public transport where it is sometimes unavoidable, physical contact with a stranger is permitted, but in such circumstances, eye contact should be avoided at all costs.

Intimacy between consenting adults is recognised as involving more touching. But that takes place behind closed doors usually with the lights out. Displays of affection in all relationships are kept to a minimum.

27

Ps and Qs

English children have their own particular catechism of accepted conduct to learn. The first rule they come across at an early age is "Mind your Ps and Qs". These have nothing to do with waiting politely to use the lavatory. Ps and Qs are short for "Pleases" and "Thank Yous". Supplication, gratitude and, most important of all, apology are central to English social intercourse, which is why English people seem to express them endlessly as if to the hard of hearing.

It is difficult for the foreigner to learn how to wield the small vocabulary necessary, but the starting point is to understand that it is almost impossible linguistically to be over grateful, over apologetic or over polite when it comes to the point. Thus, the English man or woman whose toe you tread on will be "so sorry" presumably for not having had the offending digit amputated earlier. He or she will thank you "so much" when you stop treading on it or, if you do not, ask you to with a routine of pleases and thank yous that would last any other national half a lifetime. It's just the English way.

A lack of profusion in the gratitude or apology department will certainly land anyone in such a situation in the "not very nice" camp from which there is little chance of escape.

Queuing

Foreigners look with amazement at the English queue. It is not their way of doing things at all. But for the English, queuing is a way of life.

Many still consider that one of the few plus points of the last war was the proliferation of queues. There were queues for everything. People would join one and then ask the person in front what the queue was for.

And that is the secret of English queue-mania. A queue is the one place where it is not considered bad manners to talk to a stranger without being introduced.

Such an enjoyable custom should, to the English way of thinking, commend itself naturally to all peoples. They are amazed when it does not, and do not take kindly to aliens who fail to recognise a queue when they see one ("There is a queue, you know!"), or to join in and play the queue game nicely.

Sense of Humour

The English appear to be a deeply serious people, which, by and large, they are. This gives an added piquancy to the English sense of humour. For it comes as a surprise to foreigners to find that it exists at all.

English humour, like the will-o'-the-wisp, refuses to be caught and examined and just when you think you have cracked it, you realise that you have been duped once again. For example:

Two men in a club are reading their newspapers when one says: "It says here there's a fellow in Devon who plays his cello to the seals." "Oh really", says the other. "Yes", says the first, "Of course, they don't take a blind bit of notice."

Since the English never say what they mean, often the exact opposite, and tend towards reticence and under-statement, their humour is partly based on an exaggeration of this facet of their own character. So, while in conversation they avoid confrontation, in their humour they mock that avoidance.

Tact and diplomacy are held up to ridicule in a way that would appear to give the lie to all that the English actually seem to hold dear. Thus in a popular television situation comedy, *Yes, Minister*, we are encouraged to laugh at the elaborate verbal subterfuge of the civil servant who can turn black into white and convince everyone that they were one and the same thing all the time. English humour is as much about recognition as it is about their ability to laugh at themselves, e.g:

> During a television programme on sex the audience was asked "How many people here have sex more than three times a week?" There was a weak show of hands. "And how many have sex once a month?" A sea of hands shot up. "Anyone less than that?" One man waved his arm surprisingly enthusiastically. "Once a year," he said. The audience was stunned and the interviewer observed incredulously, "You don't look very upset about it." "No," said the man, "Tonight's the night!"

Cruelty, a mainstay of German humour, has no place in its English equivalent. Not for them the acid satire of the Berlin cabarets. They prefer a gentler corrective, cleverer and more subtle.

The wry smile that greets the well-judged understatement is a characteristic English expression. They love irony and expect others to appreciate it too. In this, they are all too often disappointed as foreigners take umbrage at what appears to them to be unbearable rudeness. This, of course, merely confirms what the English have always secretly suspected – that foreigners cannot take a joke.

Obsessions

Homes...

It is largely thanks to the awful climate in England that the English lavish so much attention on their homes and gardens. They employ their leisure hours with an endless cycle of 'home improvements'. For no English home can ever be considered fully improved.

Inside and out they beaver away, installing electronic gadgets, showers, built-in furniture and turning the exterior of a suburban semi into a gothic nightmare of mullioned windows, stone-clad walls and studded front doors.

Even the family car is not safe from DIY man's attentions. He drives the impeccably polished vehicle up on to ramps, which he buys from the DIY shop, and tinkers around underneath it for hours on end.

You might think that, with all this self-servicing, self-plumbing, self-decorating and improving, English skilled labourers would be out of a job or two. But that is not the case. Sooner or later, these experts have to be called in to make good the damage caused by the over enthusiastic amateur.

Leaning back on their heels, pencils behind ears, glancing sideways and taking long breaths in between their teeth, they shake their heads. "Of course you've been fiddling with this, haven't you?" DIY man winces at 'fiddling', puts his hand ruefully into his back pocket and pays handsomely. It is tacitly understood that part of the fee buys the expert's discretion. For DIY man will still take the credit for the shower, burglar alarm or 'suping up' of the family saloon.

No disaster will ever convince the Englishman that any job is beyond him. Every job is a challenge and all challenges are to be met.

...and Gardens

Out in the garden, the English have no hesitation. They are surprisingly effective out-of-doors. Gardening is a national sport and 'green fingers' are a proudly-born English deformity.

Once they get going, something very strange happens. They temporarily lose their innate practical bias in favour of a purely personal expression.

While other nationalities tinker away with pots and potagers in an attempt to increase the foodstore and add a splash of colour, the English are landscaping – dreaming of grandiose sweeps of green, studded with plantations of exotic shrubs.

While the French content themselves with a sprinkling of mostly native plants, the English suburban garden is a riot of international flora – lilies from Tibet, wistaria from China and gunnera from Patagonia.

Garden centres thrive. Gardening magazines and books are everywhere in their houses and when the temperature indoors is below freezing, the seedlings and cuttings in the greenhouse still luxuriate in tropical warmth.

And all this in the smallest of properties, for every English garden or window box becomes a national park in the English imagination.

Railway travellers in England cannot fail to notice the numerous little collections of horticultural enclosures which cluster around embankments up and down the country. These are the allotments – municipally owned land originally leased to town dwellers in wartime to help with the production of vegetables. Even without the threat of war they are still jealously guarded patches. English men and women will wait half a lifetime to inherit one of these insalubrious little plots with their ramshackle sheds, for here they can play at being market gardeners all weekend.

For the English the first sound of spring is not really the song of the cuckoo, but the echo of the unprintable oath of the gardener who discovers that his lawn mower will not start. After that first primaeval shout, they are off. And so, throughout the summer while other people in the world are sitting outside their houses chatting, the English apply themselves to the horticultural labours of Hercules. They weed monstrous herbaceous borders, build palaeolithic rockeries, divert waters to prime fountains, cultivate giant marrows for the annual village fête and dead-head acres of asters.

If they feel in need of a change, they will go and visit someone else's garden, returning home via the garden centre with another car bootfull of plants, implements, plastic pond liners and compost.

Come rain or shine, but mostly come rain, the English mulch and prune their way through the year, rejoicing in the dignity of their labour.

The Gnome

The garden gnome is a peculiarly English phenomenon which gives a fascinating insight into the English character.

In English suburban gardens, like the classical statue in great English parks, the coarse-fishing gnome wielding his little rod is a reminder not of some pagan past but of a secret and precious time before the coming of adulthood, the very childhood the English had thought they had forgotten.

Along with coy garden poetry, a laughably impractical sundial and, above all, the Enid Blytonesque name on the garden gate – 'Bide-a-Wee', 'Dunroamin', 'Kenada' (the home of Kenneth and Ada) or 'Olcote' (Our Little Corner of This Earth) – the gnome helps to create, in a private place, a private world in which the Englishman is just a great friendly giant.

A Nice Cup of Tea

Foreigners may scoff, marketing men may try to seduce with alternatives, but the English still carry on doggedly in their devotion to what they consider to be one of the few good things ever to come from across the sea – balm for the wounds of the Empire builder.

Whilst foreigners stiffen their sinews with something stronger, the English constitution merely demands tea. They have imbued it with almost mystical curative and comforting qualities. In moments of crisis, as a remedy for shock or just at a social gathering someone will suggest tea. It is probably their only addiction.

Tea to the average English man or woman usually means Indian tea. It is served with milk and sugar and the folklore surrounding its preparation is prodigious. First the teapot has to be heated. The tea, once made, has to be left to 'stand' and 'brew' – but not so long that it becomes 'stewed'. Cold milk is poured into the bottom of each cup and then tea is added either with the addition of water or, more normally, 'just as it comes' – neat and strong.

Among the upper classes, China tea is considered smarter. Preparation rituals are similar, but milk is always added after the tea if it is taken at all. A slice of lemon is often substituted. Sugar goes in last.

In great English institutions tea brewed in vast urns like Russian samovars still often comes with milk and sugar already added. It should be approached with caution. The liquid that oozes out of the English variety is best described as canteen tea – the kind that stands up without a cup.

Leisure and Pleasure

English magazines will often advertise themselves as being devoted to sport and leisure. This is puzzling for to the English sport is seldom leisurely.

The reason they are lumped together can only be that, in English eyes, leisure activities share with sport the element of competition so essential to the English way of life. Leisure is a challenge and one must make one's own better than anyone else's.

The high flying executive who plays with model helicopters on the Common is subconsciously waiting for another high flier with similar toys to compete with. The man who cleans his car in a suburban street on a Sunday morning is really running a polishing race with his neighbours with every grunting sweep of the chamois leather.

Even a peaceful pint in the pub can easily turn into a drinking competition if the right adversary turns up.

When bad weather threatens, the English, unlike other people, do not invariably take shelter in their houses. For heavy weather is the ultimate adversary – a worthy and familiar opponent.

Wrapped from head to foot in waterproof clothing, they set out on extended hikes, best feet forward, carrying maps in little plastic bags around their necks. Up hill and down dale, the English follow vehemently protected footpaths on these route marches which they deceptively refer to as 'rambles'.

The Challenge

Uncomfortable forays of this kind are a particular English favourite. In summer months they will travel miles to the Lake District, where rain can be almost guaranteed, to pit their stamina against the worst that nature can throw at them.

So popular are these struggles against the elements that some enterprising individuals have formulated courses in physical discomfort in remote and inhospitable areas of the British Isles where other English people pay substantial fees to be assured of a serious challenge.

These courses, posing under such romantic titles as 'Survival', are pursued for their perceived character building qualities. The stiffening of upper lips is guaranteed.

English companies, sparing no expense, will send their executives away for days on end to play these games. The assumption is that a man or woman who can shine in physical adversity will also excel in stressful business struggles. It never occurs to these companies to sack all their employees and take on the men who run the courses instead.

However they justify these excesses, the fact is that the English just love a physical challenge and eschew comfort as sybaritic. Even in a potentially comfortable situation in the Mediterranean sun, they will pit their white skins against its harmful rays until the evening comes and they are thoroughly burnt.

Sports

The English are devoted to sports of all kinds. Their children have always been trained from the earliest age to take them seriously. Even today in schools up and down the country little boys and girls in shorts are exhorted to "play the game!" by their elders and betters who will come down heavily on 'slacking' whenever they see it.

Whether it be football, rugby, hockey or any other team game, they start young and carry on, barring accidents, until they have to hang up their boots and watch others doing it.

This they do with boundless enthusiasm and extremely vocally in spectator stands or from touchlines, often in sub-zero temperatures or force ten gales with the ever-present threat of a downpour. Nothing can dampen their ardour. Even at night they carry on watching in stadiums bright with floodlight.

Cricket

Cricket to the English is not just a game. It is a symbol – a twenty-two man personification of all English beliefs and philosophies. Ignore it at your peril.

If you do you could be 'on a sticky wicket'. You might then be accused of not having put your 'best foot forward' and of not 'playing a straight bat', both hallmarks of the bounder.

Cricket is the national summer pastime of the English race. Visitors to England would have to be blind not to spot at least one weekend cricket match in their travels. And even the blind cannot avoid the coverage of international matches which dribbles out of radios in every public place throughout the season. It is inescapable. On every village green or television screen, a group of men, dressed in white, stand around waiting for something to happen.

The English invented cricket 750 years ago and are fiercely proprietorial about it. Its laws are one of the great mysteries of life, passed on among the initiated in a coded language. In the past they took the game all over the world and always won. Gradually, though, other nations' teams have got better at it, until now the English stand a jolly good chance of being beaten wherever they go.

Whenever this happens, the English get very heated. They accuse everyone in sight of having cheated: of tampering with the ball by roughing up the surface (so that it behaves in an irregular fashion); of shaving the head to reduce wind-resistance on the run-in; of 'sledging' (hurling abuse at the batsman so as to put him off his stroke); of wearing the wrong clothes, and of playing too fast for a one-day match – all of which they vigorously complain is just 'not cricket'.

Games with Animals

The English adore horses and dogs to such an extent that they even involve them as partners in some of their sports. Over the centuries these animals have proved themselves admirable assistants in the eradication of foxes and specially-bred game birds.

Although they are seen as archetypally English pastimes, field or 'blood' sports have always been the pre-serve of the rich few – not for the masses. But one animal sport everyone enjoys enormously is racing horses. Wherever and whenever racing takes place, all strata of English society congregate, brought together by a common enthusiasm for that magic combination – horses, the great outdoors, and physical discomfort.

Annual Holidays

Once a year most English families take an extended holiday. Until air travel became more common these family holidays were almost always spent in one of the many English seaside resorts.

During July and August convoys of Austins, Rovers and Fords would snake their way down winding English lanes to seaside towns. Here shops on the seafront sold buckets, spades, lilos, candyfloss, toffee apples, seaside rock, risqué postcards, fish and chips and brightly-coloured canvas wind breaks.

Pitching their little camps on the beach, English families spent days on end appearing to enjoy melting ice creams, leaking thermos flasks and sand in everything.

Rain on at least half the days could be guaranteed. But then there were the delights of the seaside pier. Here the maritime race enjoyed all the sensations of going to sea without being seasick or, worse, meeting any foreigners.

Nowadays the English start their holidays at Luton, Gatwick, Stanstead, Manchester, Birmingham or Heathrow airports and fly over those winding English lanes, bound for Spain, Greece, Cyprus, Florida or almost anywhere where they can still be guaranteed amusement arcades, risqué postcards to send home, the reassuring smell of onions frying, and fish and chips.

Here they carry on just as if they were still in Bognor Regis, Blackpool or Brighton. They stick together, ignoring the existence of the natives, stake out corners of the beach and spend most of the day lying in the sun. At night they drink, dance, and throw up in discotheques thoughtfully provided for the purpose by the locals.

At the end of the holiday, the English return home with burnt noses, diarrhoea and alcohol poisoning but otherwise ready to face any challenge that life can throw at them.

Eating

The English once perceived food more as fuel for the body than as something to be enjoyed for its own sake. Consequently they never really applied themselves to the art of cooking, until they became aware of the sheer awfulness of their own cuisine.

Of course it is not all dust and ashes. The rest of the world does acknowledge the supremacy of the great English breakfast (chosen from bacon, eggs, sausages, grilled tomatoes, mushrooms, potatoes, kippers, kedgeree and so on) and French chefs tacitly compliment them on their 'rosbif' which is found the world over. Universally acclaimed, too, are their puddings – steamed jam roll and apple crumble. The unwary should take care with 'Yorkshire' and 'black' puddings. Neither is quite what it seems. The first is baked batter eaten with roast beef, and the second a ferocious blood sausage, taken, by the brave, at breakfast.

On the whole, England has always been, culinarily speaking, the underdog. The puritan backlash is ever present. 'Good plain cooking' and 'honest simple fare' continue to be held in semi-religious awe in many quarters, with the clear implication that complicated and pretty dishes are neither good nor honest.

Nevertheless, continental habits have insinuated themselves, not least in the matter of eating out. Restaurants have proliferated and, as the interest in foreign food has grown, so have the choices. The supremacy of French and Italian fare is now challenged by others – Thai, Chinese, Mexican, Spanish, Russian, American.

There are even restaurants specialising in English food. One highly successful example in London calls itself 'School Dinners'. There tired and overwrought businessmen can go and enjoy such nursery fare as rice pudding and 'spotted dick' all served by well-developed girls wearing school uniforms.

Drinking

The English have been accused of starting life two drinks behind the rest of the world. This is a shame, for they have an extraordinary expertise in the matter of alcoholic beverages.

While the charge of sophistication has never been levelled at English food, the English have consumed it for hundreds of years accompanied by a bewildering range of the world's finest wines.

The best ones from France have always been shipped over the Channel in bulk for the English to drink and enjoy. For centuries they have imported the lion's share of Portugal's port and Spain's sherry in addition to brewing their own pale imitations of them.

Of the more successful native English drinks, English ale has now been partially eclipsed in popularity by lighter lagers from the Continent and the antipodes. But for years beer was one of the country's greatest sources of pride and even today there is still a sizeable number of local breweries producing regional beers which are sold extensively in pubs up and down the land.

The catalogue of English alcoholic triumphs continues with London Gin. This is drunk all over the world along with Indian (English Imperial) tonic water and provides the base for thousands of cocktails. Whisky, of course, comes from Scotland but the English consider it peculiarly their own, keeping the choicest malts for themselves, perhaps because they do not want the rest of the world to get more than two drinks ahead of them.

What is Sold Where

Until a few years ago the English used to shop at their local greengrocer, butcher, baker and so on. Now these small shops have all but capitulated as their customers pile into their cars and get everything they need at huge out-of-town-centre hangars filled with all their hearts' desires.

The only shops to have survived the march of the supermarkets in any numbers are the corner shops, known in some quarters as 'Patelleries' since so many of them are run by Ugandan Asian immigrant families. These corner shops are often supermarkets in miniature and sell anything from sweets to sweat bands, nappies to newspapers. Many of them are also open all day and half the night.

In all this cultural upheaval, there appears to be only one golden rule. You can get anything you need in very small or very big shops and nothing in medium-sized ones.

Health and Hygiene

The French are fascinated by their livers, the Germans by their digestive systems and the Spanish by their blood. To the English, none of these have anything like the appeal of the bowels.

From earliest childhood, the English are brought up to take a keen interest in the regularity and consistency of their bowel movements. The day that does not start with a satisfactory visit to the lavatory starts on the wrong foot, and the English child who fails in this morning duty is deemed to show signs of 'crankiness' or to have 'got out of bed on the wrong side'. It is a preoccupation that lasts for life.

While their continental neighbours breakfast on pastries and jam, the English tuck in to bowls of cereal, rich in fibre and advertising their efficacy through such names as 'Force' or 'All Bran'.

Correctives for bowel disorders throng English bathroom shelves and old-fashioned remedies continue to sell well. 'Carter's Little Liver Pills' promise to cure 'that out-of-sorts feeling due to constipation'. 'Califig – Syrup of Figs' is billed as an effective laxative for all the family. Both are less violent and unpleasant than their no-nonsense rival in shirt-sleeves – good old-fashioned Castor Oil.

To correct the effects of over-indulgence in one of the above preparations, 'looseness' as the English term it, there is another splendid proprietary medicine. The origins of 'J. Collis Browne's Chlorodyne' have become obscured by time. The good doctor's patients obviously got about a bit. One of the ecstatic endorsements accompanying his little bottles boasts: "I have even used chlorodyne with great effect on Mont Blanc."

Reasonably steady on home ground, English bowels suffer exquisitely abroad. Thanks to the appalling nature of local food and water, the English traveller constantly runs into bowel problems. From 'Delhi-belly' to 'Montezuma's Revenge' or 'The Aztec Quickstep' they strike him or her in every far-flung corner of the earth.

Many of the English juggle with laxatives and binding agents all their lives in the hope of one day returning to that blissful childhood state when an adult would nod approvingly at the first droppings of the day. For many of them this faecal nirvana is never reached.

None of them can be persuaded to flirt with the ubiquitous suppository so beloved of Europeans. While the French will even treat a headache with one, the English doctor their bowels with pills and prunes.

With more serious illnesses, the English are at their most stoic. Not for them the wailing and gnashing of teeth heard in foreign hospitals. Fortitude in the face of adversity is the thing. Remember Queen Victoria's dying words: "I feel a little better..."

Hygiene

When it comes to hygiene, the English are traditionally inclined. Showers are gaining in popularity but in most English houses the bath still reigns supreme.

Whilst the rest of the world looks on horrified, the English wallow in baths filled with their own dirt and diluted with warm water. But then they do use more soap than any other nation, which, as far as they are concerned, counts for a lot. For as every English person knows, other nations, especially the French, just put on more scent when they start to smell.

Custom and Tradition

The English are a deeply nostalgic people and value customs and traditions above almost everything. It does not seem to matter just where traditions have come from or why they have survived. They are traditions, and that is enough for them.

The rest of the world accepts and quite enjoys the outward trappings of this English trait. Thousands of people fly into London every year to watch traditional jamborees such as the Changing of the Guard or the State Opening of Parliament.

Tradition, to the English, represents continuity, which must be preserved at all costs.

Family Gatherings

Though they are the least family-orientated people on earth, the English would not dream of spending their Christmas anywhere else but in the vipers' nest they refer to as the 'bosom of the family'. This annual festival almost always ends in tears and to get over it takes many families a good six months.

But tradition rules and, come September, English families are beginning to plan for another family Christmas, having apparently completely forgotten the mayhem of the one before.

Christmas apart, family members avoid each other religiously throughout the year except on compulsory occasions such as christenings, weddings and funerals. Of these, funerals and christenings, being the shortest, are the most popular. Weddings are only distinguishable from pitched battles by the uniforms of the participants.

Planning for these nightmare events starts early, as do the arguments. Even though English etiquette books try to help by pointing out who is responsible for organising and paying for the bride's dress, the flowers, the church, the choir, the organist, the cars, the reception, the food, the photographers and St. John's Ambulance, the English will fight furiously on every single issue for months before, right through and even after the great day.

It came as no surprise to many survivors of similar occasions to read the newspaper report of the bride's father who initiated legal proceedings against his son-in-law's parents (about who should pay what) while the 'happy couple' were still on their honeymoon.

It is the triumph of English hope over English experience that these gatherings ever take place at all.

For Queen and Country

Fighting is one of the things that the English do best. Over the centuries, they have confronted almost every race on the planet at one time or another. Naturally, they have become rather good at it.

Nobody can curb English pugnacity. It is in their blood, and displays of ritualised ferocity are even seen as socially desirable and glamorous.

Nearly a century after the armies of all other countries became entirely fighting machines, the English still keep several large bodies of men from mainly aristocratic families in barracks in London. One of the major duties of these men is to dress up in period costume from time to time and march about the streets looking fierce.

Once a year, these same men meet on a large parade ground and do quite a lot of marching about and looking fierce in front of the current monarch. In this they are accompanied by noisy wind bands playing mostly German music.

When it actually comes to war, the English are extraordinarily tenacious once they get going. Images of London under the blitz reinforce their perception of their own indomitability, and the lack of proper equipment and a shortage of men are never seen as a handicap. Remember Dunkirk.

And it is not only in formal battle conditions that the English snap to attention. Their natural bellicosity is, at all times, just below the surface. The work started by away teams led by Raleigh and Drake is continued by the supporters of English football squads. It seems they have a fundamental need to prove their physical superiority not merely to each other but to others. Despite this, England alone of the major countries in Europe, indeed the world, has abolished military conscription with all the opportunities it affords for formalised aggression.

Religion

The English are not a deeply religious race. Hundreds of years ago they decided that Roman Catholicism with its teachings about original sin and the unworthiness of the human race could not really have been meant for them. So they designed a church of their own – the Church of England.

Attendance at church services is not obligatory and, indeed, not a widespread habit. Membership, on the other hand, is assumed to be the norm and English bureaucratic forms with their inquiries about religion mirror the national attitude to the rest of Christendom with their query: "If not C of E, state, 'other'."

The broader purpose of religion in England is to inculcate in the natives a system of morals and behaviour loosely seen as Christian but more specifically as English. Originally born out of the desperation of Henry VIII to get a divorce, the Church now officially holds marriage sacrosanct and may well have to reinvent itself if another monarch wishes to emulate its founder.

In English eyes, the Church is made for man and not the other way about. Holding fast to this belief, they are probably the most tolerant race on earth when it comes to the beliefs of others. Mosques, chapels, synagogues and temples abound in England and they cannot understand why the rest of the world feels so passionately about something which is, for them, essentially a diversion.

Culture

England is the country of Shakespeare, Milton, Byron and Beatrix Potter. The first is, by common consent, a hero of the human race, a Titan of literature against whom all other writers in the world over the past four hundred years have been measured. The second two are worthy names in most literate households. But the work of the fourth is best known to the English; for while the first three tended to write about people, Beatrix Potter wrote about animals and the English prefer animals and understand them better.

So it is that a mention of Peter Rabbit, Mrs Tiggy-Winkle and Jeremy Fisher elicit an immediate response from English audiences while the agonies of Hamlet, Coriolanus and Othello leave the better read of them intellectually stimulated but emotionally stone-cold.

Other nations may thrill to Henry V's call to arms at Agincourt or warm to Juliet's tearful pleas to her Romeo, but English audiences of all ages reach for the tissues on hearing how Jemima Puddleduck outwits the fox, adjusts her bonnet and escapes the cooking pot to live another sunny day.

Close on the heels of Beatrix Potter comes the sinister A.A. Milne, whose *Winnie The Pooh* – written by an adult for other adults but passed off as a children's book – is read by adults for the rest of their lives.

Paradise Lost, sadly deficient in the fauna department, stays firmly between its covers.

Television

For the majority of English, watching television is their only real experience of a broader 'culture'.

English television, naturally, majors in sports coverage and titanic struggles occur between television companies to win exclusive rights to televise the most popular games. But even the English cannot quite live by sport alone. Pandering to the competitive nature of their audiences, broadcasters screen large numbers of quiz and games shows. In addition they produce a wealth of news and discussion programmes and the occasional original drama series. These are bulked out with a staggering number of imported and specially-created soap operas and mini-series, which are hugely popular. For the rest, it is old films of which the English never tire.

Programmes aimed at the more intellectual members of English society are screened late at night so as to cause the least inconvenience to the majority.

The Press

The average Frenchman travelling to work reads a novel, the English read newspapers. Their voracious appetite for printed news, gossip and scandal is unequalled and the English newspaper market has attracted entrepreneurs from all over the world who struggle to the death to obtain the proprietorship of one of the chunks of it.

Nobody really understands why. The press cannot

hope to compete for immediacy of coverage with radio and television. Perhaps it is because the English prefer their news, like their climate – cold. Or perhaps it is because they secretly believe that anything viewed in retrospect is really more real.

The Arts

The English theatre today is mainly supported by block bookings for new productions of old musicals or for the latest Andrew Lloyd Webber spectacular. These the English will pay for. When Lloyd Webber meets Beatrix Potter, nobody will be able to get a seat.

With the cinema, things are a little more encouraging. Rumours of its total demise thirty years ago turned out to have been somewhat exaggerated, and even foreign films are seen by thousands in English cinemas every week. But then the English do love an 'outing'.

Dragging their children behind them they will visit museums and art galleries to rub shoulders with foreign visitors and buy souvenirs and reproductions of famous paintings.

When it comes to art appreciation, the English tend to be nervous, suspecting that they are not all that good at it. On the whole they tend towards the taste of Queen Victoria, showing a marked preference for large paintings of people and animals by artists like Landseer. If the picture tells a story, so much the better. If they cannot understand it, they tend to dismiss it.

Fundamentally, the English see themselves more in the role of patrons than of artists. For most of them culture is a luxury and too much luxury is a dangerous thing.

Systems

Tradition governs almost everything the English do. And when it comes to the systems by which the country is run, English traditions are at their most enduring.

Public Transport

It is a tradition that trains generally do not run on time unless the passenger is two minutes late. It is also a tradition that, although the price of railway travel is infinitely variable, concessionary rates are only available at times or days other than those on which one wishes to travel.

But with all its inadequacies, the English railway system is one facet of the English life that is imbued with more than its fair share of English sentiment. Anoraked train spotters, those archetypal eccentrics, still abound. Deep in the English psyche there is still a vague memory of a golden age of railway travel when E. Nesbit's *Railway Children* waved their petticoats at the train driver, thus averting disaster.

English urban buses travel in convoys so as to ensure that passengers wait as long as possible at the bus stops. Then, just before fighting breaks out among the waiting hordes, three or four buses sporting the same number will heave into view. It is always a feast or a famine.

Whatever transport you choose you will find that, in England, you are nearly always late. This is because, contrary to popular belief, the English are not punctual by nature. It is considered polite to arrive a few minutes after the time you were invited for. English transport will probably ensure that you do anyhow. It's all part of the system.

The Open Road

Cars are among the favourite status symbols of the English. Consequently there are far too many of them on English roads, as any driver will tell you.

Almost every English man and woman over the age of seventeen either owns or has access to a car and uses it often. This leads to enormous traffic and parking problems in towns and to terminal motorway congestion. But the English are undeterred even if they often spend whole Bank Holidays in their cars in traffic jams.

Observant foreigners are quick to spot that the English, unlike other people in the world, drive on the left – a habit they often find hard to kick when driving abroad. Driving on the left is traditional and therefore, to the English, indisputably right.

By and large, the English are well-behaved on the roads. They use their horns sparingly and give way to each other at crossroads.

Punctilious in their observation of traffic signs, they will wait for ever at traffic-light-controlled pedestrian crossings even if there are no pedestrians in sight. If there are any, they screech to a halt and wait patiently for them to cross the road. This comes as a surprise to foreigners who are used to crossing themselves on the pavement before running like hares across the highway.

A Good Education

For English children whose parents can afford it, school often means a public (which really means private) school and frequently means boarding. The English approve of boarding schools. They believe that children develop better away from home. Although there are some mixed public schools, many are single-sex establishments, where pupils have the opportunity of experiencing some aspects of the monastic or prison existence at an early stage in their lives.

The alternative is the State system with its free public (which really means public) day schools. But whether state or private, the emphasis is still on 'a good education', for the feeling is that life and all its glories will thereafter be yours for the asking.

It all comes down to tradition, like so many things in the English way of life, and traditionally 'you get what you pay for'. The implication is clear. If you are not paying, you are not getting much.

Crime and Punishment

The English policeman (or woman) on the beat who can be asked the way or the time and who will always give a civil answer really does exist.

To a world that is more used to gun-toting law enforcement officers who might know the way to the nearest park but are certainly not about to tell you, the English police person is a curiosity.

Serried ranks of them attend every open air occasion and provide a comforting sense of continuity. They are always on hand everywhere except, as the English observe, when you really need one.

Unlike their European and transatlantic counterparts, they will never fine you on the spot and will seldom use unnecessary violence. They will just caution or arrest you and turn up in court to tell the judge and full supporting cast exactly why you should be fined, imprisoned or deported.

The English expect their police to be beyond reproach and are shocked to the core when charges of brutality or corruption come to light, despite the fact that such behaviour is the stuff of many police dramas on television. As far as the English are concerned, life should never imitate art. They seem to have no difficulty accepting the one while rejecting the other and go on to be shocked all over again when yet another ugly truth is revealed.

Prison

English prisons are, by common consent, overcrowded and ill-equipped. Prisoners quickly learn what crime is really all about and reformed characters are pretty thin on the ground.

The English are becoming increasingly aware of the shortcomings of their prison system and are looking closely at other countries' practices and performances.

Meanwhile one ex-public schoolboy, imprisoned for fraud, is on record as having observed that his school education turned out to have been a perfect preparation for the rigours of prison life, except that in prison he was marginally more comfortable.

Law

English law, like many aspects of English life, is based on precedence.

Loosely constructed on the principles of right and wrong the system is impenetrable to the average citizen and quite alien to most foreigners.

It is acted out in real-life drama in period costume as the judiciary, the guilty and the innocent juggle with truth and falsehood in a courageous attempt to find either. And then, if a prisoner's guilt is established, to make the punishment fit the crime. It is the proud boast of the English legal system that this sometimes happens.

Government and Bureaucracy

The English like to believe they are ruled by consent. They have a well-developed sense of personal freedom and, whatever the realities of the situation, have to feel that they are the masters of their own fate. They do not take kindly to control of any sort and insist on the fiction that they do so only on a voluntary basis.

When it comes to bureaucracy, the English view it as a necessary evil. Their innate concern that 'things are done properly' inclines them to accept yards and yards of red tape whilst their natural instinct for directness as well as their love of complaining incline them to reject it.

English bureaucracy and English red tape, like everything else English, are perceived as being the best of their kind in the world and definitely boulevards ahead of anything Europe has to offer.

Politics

Politics for the English is largely a gentle game: a rearranging of the deck chairs on the Titanic. Not for them the unseemly riots and histrionics of foreign parliaments.

To the English, politicians are not to be trusted. They are out for their own ends and only there to be despised. Only when compared to the politicians of other countries, and those of Brussels in particular, do they have any saving graces.

Nevertheless, when it comes to General Elections, many English men and women turn out to vote as a matter of course. Most of them vote according to family traditions but a few occasionally change horses which keeps everyone in government on their toes for a few weeks.

Deep down the English are a conservative bunch and do not like change, which is just as well because they seldom get it.

In the Mother of Parliaments at Westminster (in a building designed in the last century to look five hundred years old) English politicians carry on their business with much historical pageantry and partially in period costume. Continuity and pugnacity mingle here too as witness the recent reincarnation of Boadicea – Warrior Queen of the Iceni – who made the fatal mistake of going one confrontation too far. For, as every English person knows, it is not only 'all for one' but also 'one for all'. English solidarity finally finds the English back-to-back looking outwards. Rather like musical chairs, you must not risk ending up outside the circle.

When it comes to the home front they recognise the overwhelming danger from outside which always threatens to destroy their way of life. Cold shoulder is fundamentally to cold shoulder even across political divides.

It is this common sense of the threat from over the sea that has been responsible for the fact that there has never been a unified English revolution. Even when everyone else in the world was having one, the English resisted it. Revolution, then as now, would have meant backs being turned on the Channel with the certainty of their being stabbed by the wily French.

This dearth of any real social upheaval has resulted in a staggering lack of change in the English way of life.

Typically the English have made a virtue out of even that necessity and it is reflected in their politics. It is no accident that the political scene in England is dominated by two political parties called not Republicans, Democrats, Christian Democrats, Solidarity or any other namby-pamby names but Conservative and Labour. The former echoes the unchanging quality of English life. The latter, the Puritan work ethic with its dignification of labour for its own sake.

There is, of course, a third political group – the Liberals. They just chose completely the wrong name on both counts and start with a crippling disadvantage. Changing it to Liberal Democrats was yet another step in the wrong direction. They may never achieve power.

Business

To the rest of the world English business people still have a somewhat amateur air. They seem to prefer to rely on an instinctive approach to business, mistrusting foreign methods of analysis and working. This makes them slightly out of their depth in the global business arena.

Some of the more courageous members of the English business community are trying to push their colleagues forward with fighting talk about not being left behind. You can recognise these brave souls by their personal fax machines, portable telephones and lapel badges at international exhibitions. Not for them the horror of isolation.

They are in touch with everyone at all times and in all time zones. How long it will take for them to get the rest of their compatriots connected remains to be seen.

The English have been characteristically cautious when dealing with Europe. Some small comfort was afforded by the community's original appellation 'the Common Market' with its implication of 'common-ness', and therefore, dismissability. Subsequent re-christenings of itself have been predictably slow to catch on in England where the idea of a European Union is still considered with deep suspicion and undisguised distaste. Few are prepared to jump into the water. Like timorous bathers, they prefer to hover on the brink until someone they can really trust tells them that "It's lovely once you're in". The problem is, whom can they believe?

Getting By

In English business practice operations are characterised by an unusual devotion to democracy. Since individual decision making is considered dangerous, almost every decision is taken by committee. So much so, that whenever you try to get hold of an English business man or woman, you will invariably be told that he or she is 'in a meeting'. Here they will sit trying to reach consensus in preference to a decision.

The popularly held belief that the English work harder than other people took a hammering when a report showed that, on average, the Germans work 44.9 hours a week, the Italians 42.4 and the English 42. The English, of course, pointed out that both the Germans and the Italians have more holidays and that anyhow, it is not the quantity but the quality of work that counts.

They also pride themselves fiercely on their ability to 'muddle through', that is to act without too much worry about discipline or planning. In the past this attitude has served them well, and the past holds all the lessons the English wish to learn.

In Good Company

English companies are still largely organised on traditional lines. That is to say, they are based on the concept of a many layered pyramid – a vertical chain of command from the Chairman and Managing Director at the top to the humblest employee at the bottom.

This mirrors the class structure at the heart of the English way of life and indeed many of the tenets of 'well-bred' behaviour still subsist in business etiquette. For although the English are naturally distrustful and suspicious when it comes to business, they appear to be prepared to put their faith and indeed their money into a bargain sealed with nothing more than a handshake. Stranger still, it seems to work.

Just Obeying Orders

The English do not like being told what to do. Any order has to be given with a degree of politeness which many other nations find incomprehensible.

Should you follow custom and express an order as a request, you will achieve the desired effect. Express it simply as an order, with no hint of personal choice, and the English will invariably break for tea.

Conversation and Gestures

In conversation the English are at their most obtuse. For they hardly ever say what they mean, and very often say the exact opposite.

Thus when you are telling a story to an Englishman or woman which elicits the response: "How interesting!", it should not be taken at face value. Faint praise damns as surely as criticism.

When an English man or woman enquires about the health of another, it will invariably elicit the response: "Mustn't grumble!" This is English hypocrisy writ large. For grumbling is a national pastime. They love to find fault, and no aspect of their lives escapes their venom. Their health, the Government, bureaucracy, the price of food, young people, old people – all are grist to their mill. Nodding sagely and united in discontent, they lay into anything and everything. And finally, refreshed by a good grumbling session, they unite in the moaners' amen – "Typical!"

Conversational Triggers

Conversation does not come easily to the English. For this reason they have developed a bewildering battery of metaphors with which even the least educated English man or woman is familiar and comfortable. These include euphemisms for the avoidance of verbal confrontation with 'tricky' subjects. Thus the English do not die, they 'pass over', 'pass on', 'shuffle off' or merely 'go'. When they relieve themselves they 'spend a penny', 'wash their hands' or 'answer the call'.

They are devoted to a huge range of hackneyed expressions which they drag out frequently to keep the conversational ball in play or to cover their escape. Because they are slightly ashamed of the triteness of these, they refer to them dismissively in French as 'clichés'. Moving from one to another, the skilful user will defy categorisation and avoid taking a stance on any subject under discussion. Finally he or she will tell you that "time and tide wait for no man" before leaving the field.

Foreigners can never quite get the hang of this – partly because to the English these phrases are so familiar that they are not usually quoted in full. Meteorological clichés are particularly familiar and, as such, never completed. So "it's an ill wind...", "it never rains...", "every cloud..." and so on tumble one upon the other and only the English know just how little they all really mean.

Distancing themselves from any confrontation, they will play down any anger or enthusiasm they may feel in a way which is satisfyingly maddening to foreigners. They have even evolved a special vocabulary for the purpose. One of the stars in this particular firmament is the poisonous little word 'nice'.

Niceness

'Nice' is the most overworked word in the English language whose meaning can only be divined by its context.

Being essentially non-specific and uncontentious, it can be used on any occasion to convey a response generally tending towards non-committal approval of anything from the weather to working practices.

In its negative form – 'not very nice' – it describes habits as diverse as nose-picking and cannibalism.

The English grow up with 'nice'. As children they are

warned off antisocial behaviour with the reprimand "Nice boys (or girls) don't do that!" and by the time they totter into their first conversations, they can use the word with deadly effect.

They may even imitate their elders by using it sarcastically – a favourite ploy – to put down bad behaviour: "That's nice! That's very nice!", when the tone of voice says it all. Sarcasm, the heavier the better, is very much part of the English conversational stock in trade.

English Weather

Without the topic of the weather, the English would be without one of the most useful weapons in their conversational armoury.

Rather like the inhabitants, the weather in the British Isles is particularly unpredictable. The geographic location of the country makes it naturally prey to momentary atmospheric changes, and forward planning of any outdoor event is fraught with dangers.

The English have, of course, lived with this situation for hundreds of years. Nevertheless, it appears that the changeability of the weather always takes them by surprise. If it snows, the country's transport systems grind immediately to a halt while negotiations are made to import snow-ploughs from abroad. In the spring, flash flooding annually drives householders up on to their roofs, and the innocent falling leaves of autumn cause the railways to seize up completely.

But while late frosts kill cherished plants and cloudbursts wash away the tea tents at village fêtes in high summer, they have, in English eyes, a higher purpose – to furnish conversation. The weather is not just their preferred conversational topic, it is their favourite gripe. If it is hot, it is always 'too hot'. If it is cold, it is 'freezing'.

Of course it is all so much mouth music and you can bet that the English man or woman you are talking to is merely marking conversational time and either planning an escape route or a deadly verbal thrust. Meanwhile, like a Sumo wrestler sizing up an opponent, he or she will use the weather as a foil before moving in for the kill or out of the ring.

Gestures

The English view the use of hand gestures in communication with deep suspicion. Fluttering hands and supple wrists are, to them, sure signs of theatricality (insincerity), effeminacy or foreign extraction.

English hands are usually kept firmly to English sides in all conversation. But they should be in sight at all times. It is considered very bad manners to talk to anyone with the hands in the pockets, as if preparing an instrument of aggression or silently counting loose change.

The average English man or woman will usually only use hand gestures when they are absolutely necessary such as for pointing the way (index finger of the right hand extended) or for making a forceful suggestion about your next move (index and middle fingers of the right hand raised vertically). This offensive gesture was first used, predictably, on the French by English archers at Agincourt when standing just beyond the arrow's reach to indicate that they still had their bow fingers which if they were captured, the French cut off. The gesture survives to this day – a physical expression of the English attitude towards others.

The Author

Antony Miall was born in the Lake District but migrated south at the age of nine months. He spent his childhood in Royal Tunbridge Wells where he had ample opportunity to observe the English at their most characteristic.

Apart from a brief spell in an educational establishment in one of the northern home counties, he has spent his life safely south of the Thames within easy reach of the Mediterranean.

Despite 'a good education', he has never quite qualified in Englishness. Among the subjects he is unable to get to grips with are discomfort and moderation. Not naturally competitive, he has nevertheless strenuously defended the right of others to follow all types of sport, especially on Saturday afternoons when he likes to have the shops to himself.

In addition to shopping his enthusiasms include playing the piano better than he thought he could. This he has done several times on concert platforms, on the radio and on television. He also enjoys seeing his name in print and has written several books on Victorian songs and society, which he studied during the breaks between music lectures.

Bringing his talents to bear on a career as a public relations consultant, he has handled a surprising number of clients in many fields. Still looking for the ideal occupation, he is seeking a challenging opening for an ambitious, competitive, thrusting executive (for a friend) and a highly paid non-executive position with plenty of travel to warm countries for himself.

Once happily married, he is now just happily in Wandsworth, has one daughter, two cats and a very significant other.